Contents

ISBN 0-7935-4092-5

HAL•LEONARD®
CORPORATION
7777 W. BLUEMOUND RD. P.O. BOX 13819 MILWAUKEE, WI 53213

Visit Hal Leonard Online at
www.halleonard.com

Boy Meets Horn

Registration 4
Rhythm: Swing

By Duke Ellington,
Irving Mills and Rex Stewart

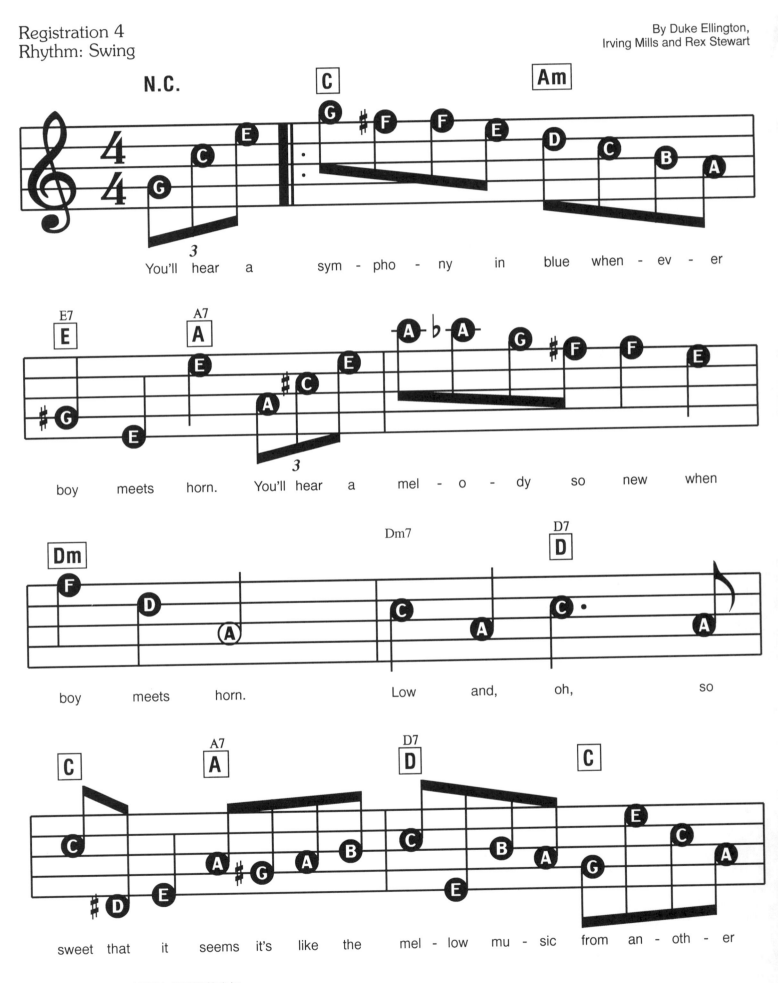

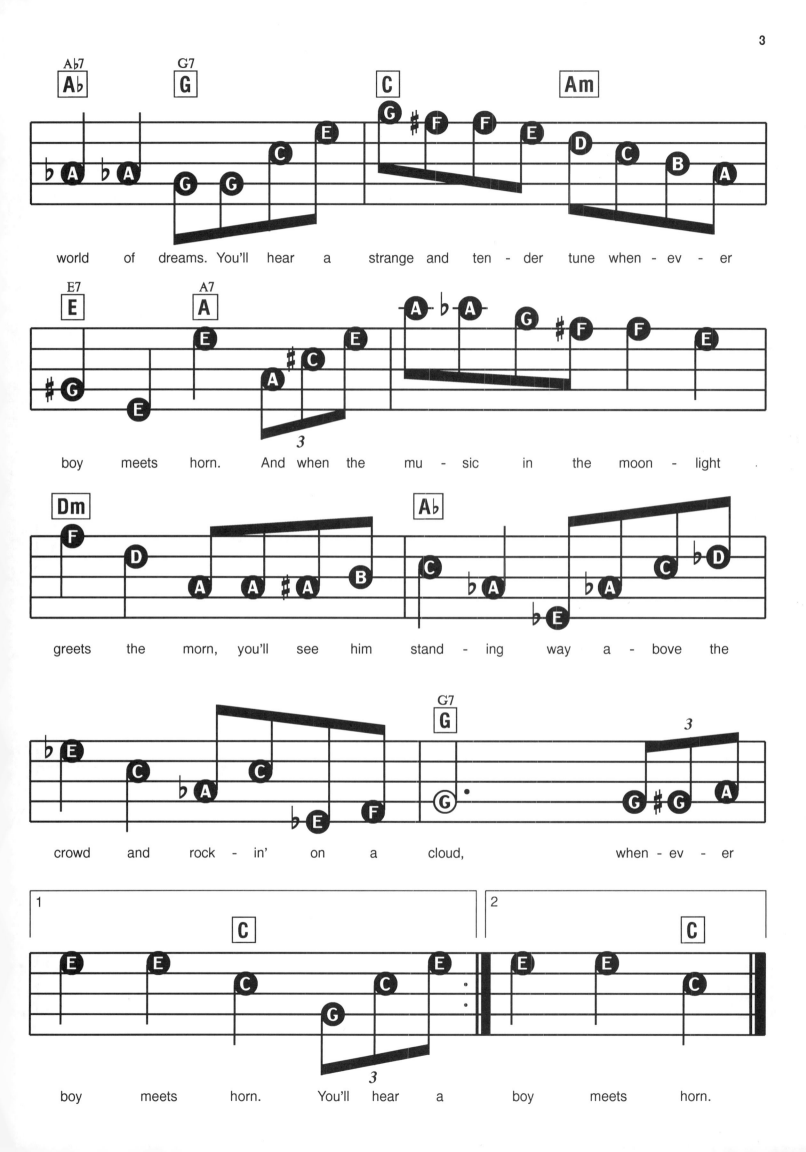

C-Jam Blues

Registration 7
Rhythm: Swing

By Duke Ellington

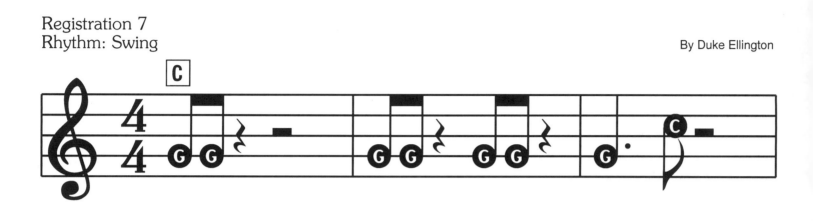

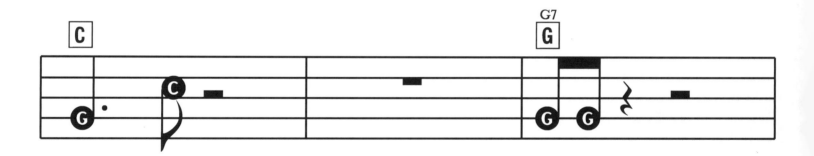

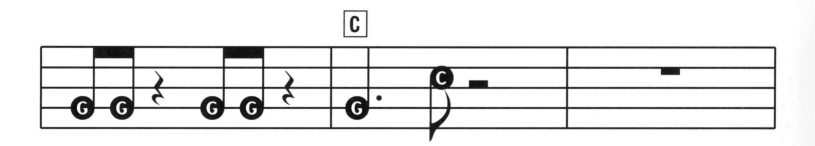

5

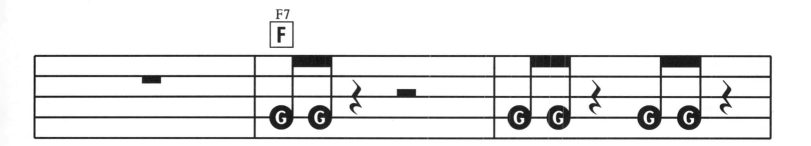

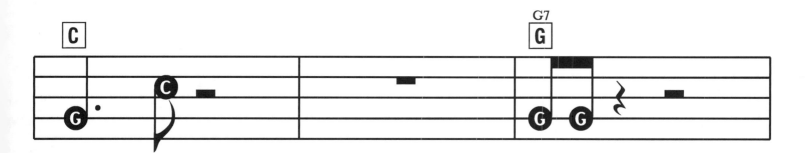

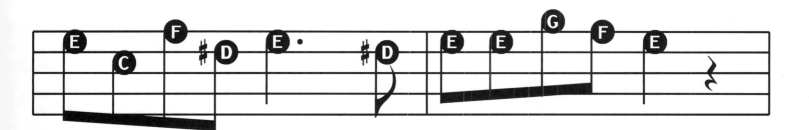

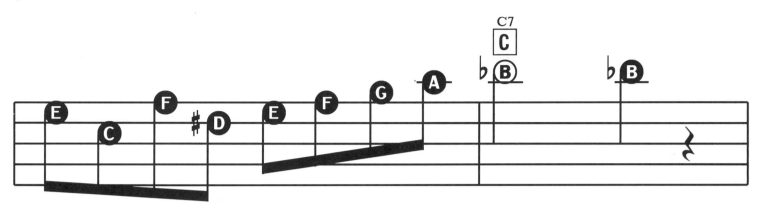

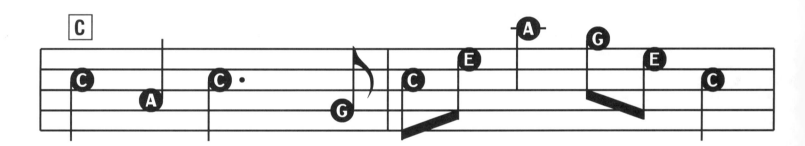

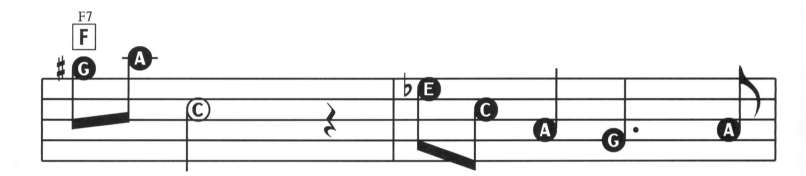

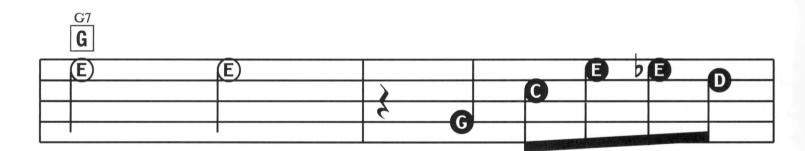

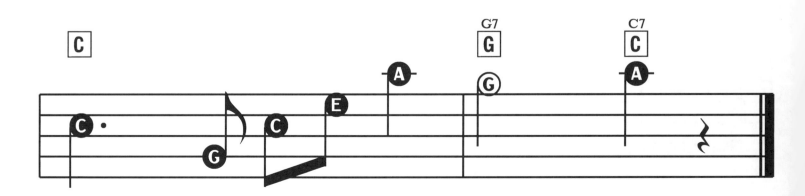

The Creole Love Call

Registration 7
Rhythm: Fox Trot or Swing

Words by Billy Strayhorn
Music by Duke Ellington

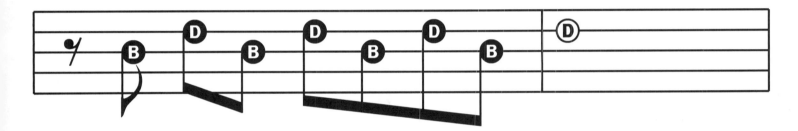

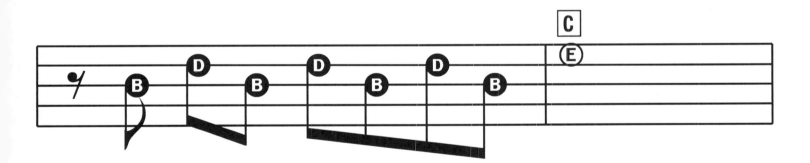

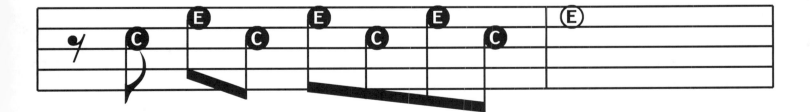

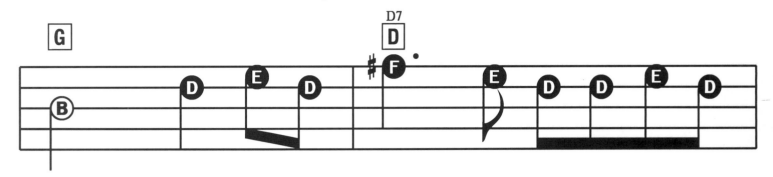

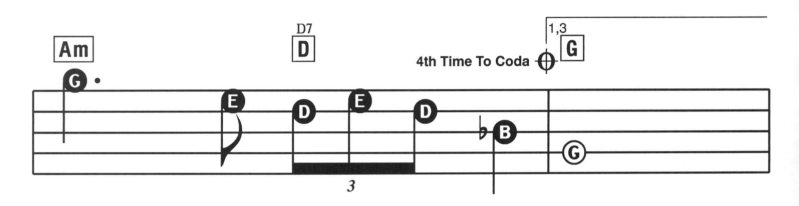

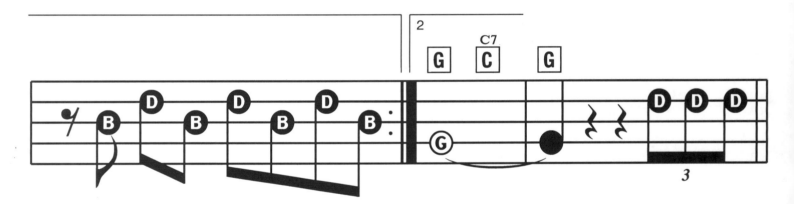

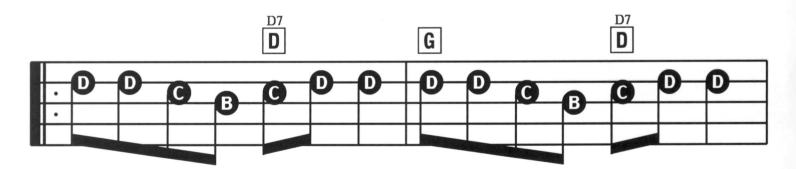

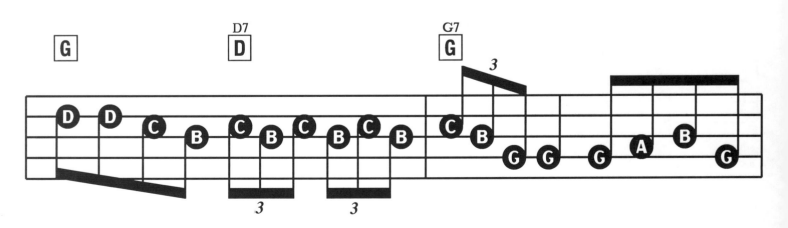

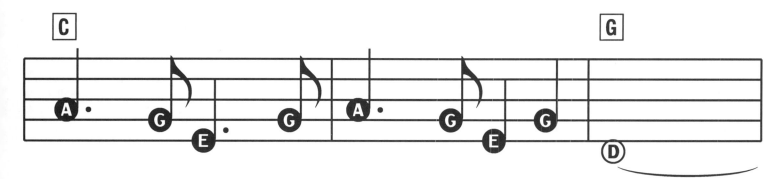

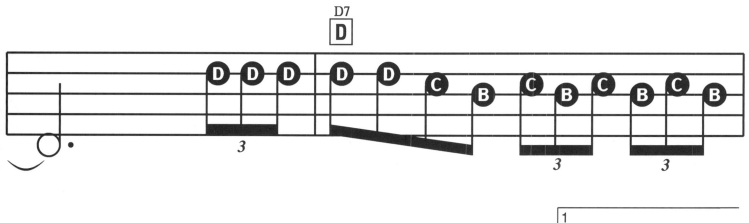

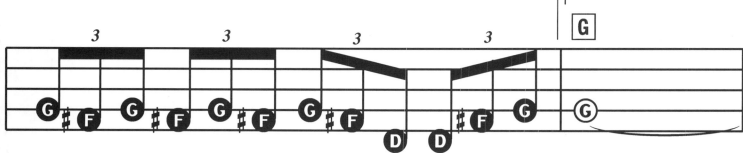

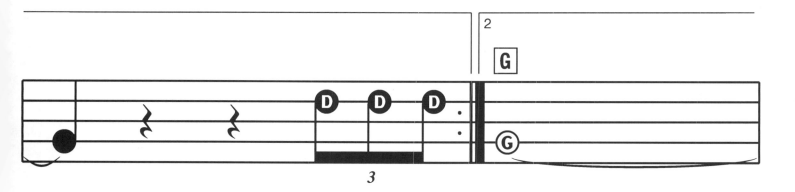

D.S. al Coda
(Return to %
Play to ⊕ and
Skip to Coda)

CODA

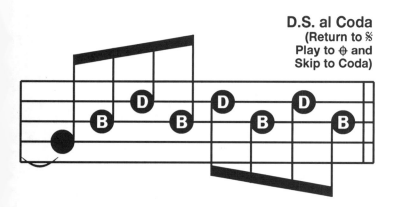

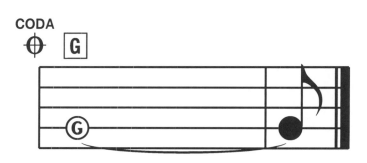

Caravan

Registration 7
Rhythm: Ballad or Fox Trot

Words and Music by Duke Ellington,
Irving Mills and Juan Tizol

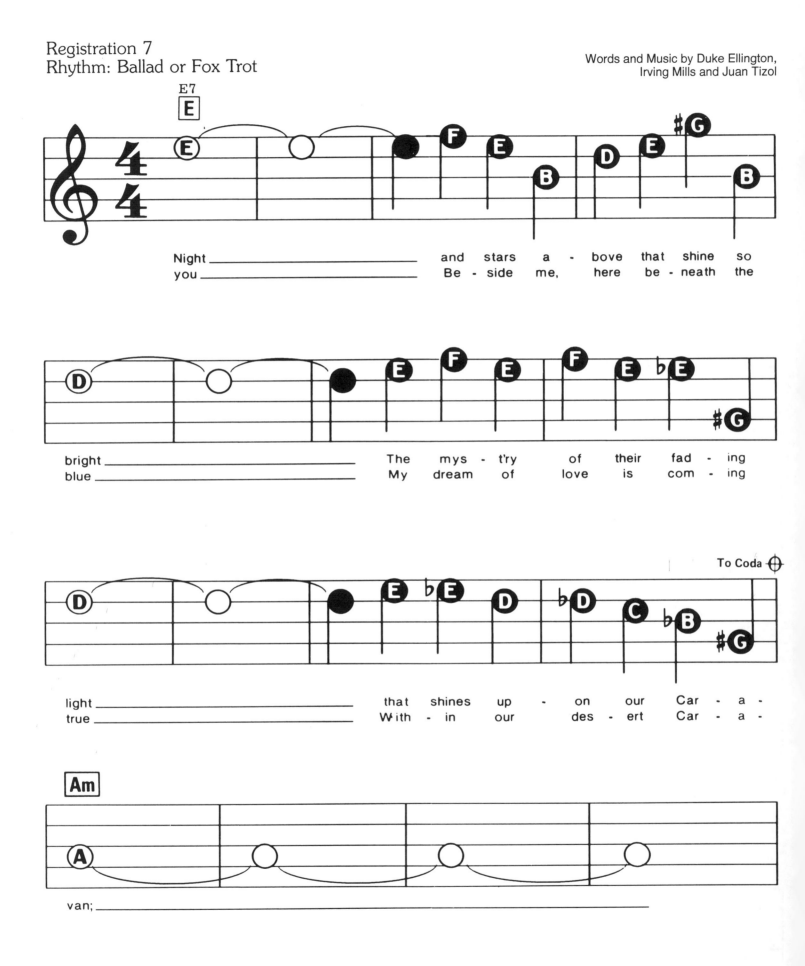

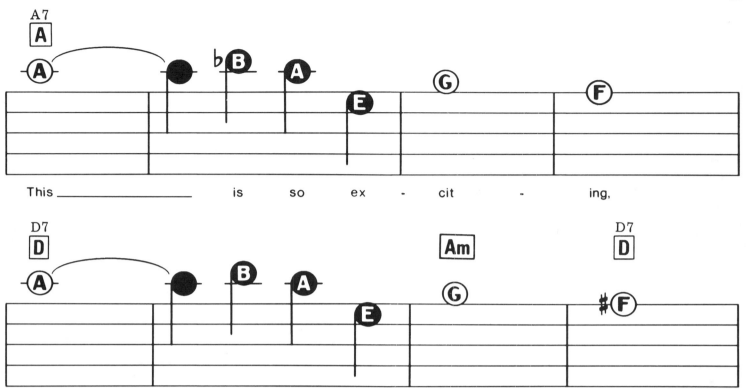

This _____ is so ex - cit - ing,

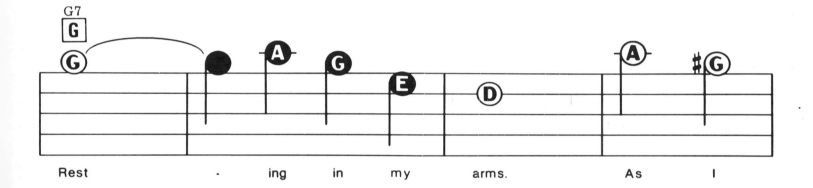

You _____ are so in - vit - ing,

Rest - ing in my arms. As I

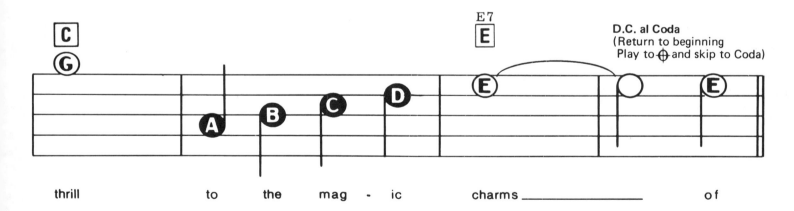

D.C. al Coda
(Return to beginning
Play to ⊕ and skip to Coda)

thrill to the mag - ic charms _____ of

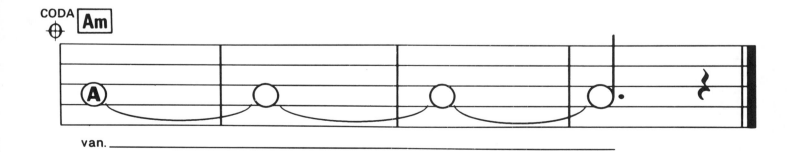

van. _____

Cotton Tail

Registration 4
Rhythm: Swing

By Duke Ellington

Day Dream

Registration 3
Rhythm: Ballad

Words by John Latouche
Music by Duke Ellington and Billy Strayhorn

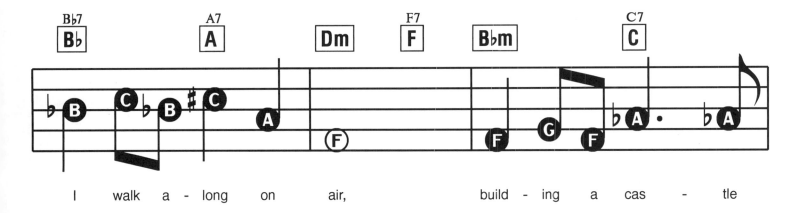

I walk a - long on air, build - ing a cas - tle

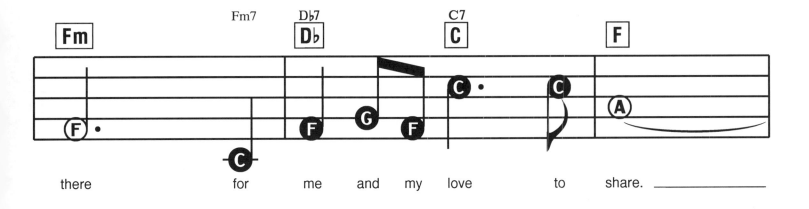

there for me and my love to share. _____

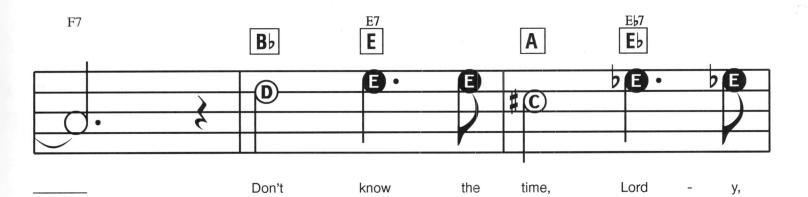

_____ Don't know the time, Lord - y,

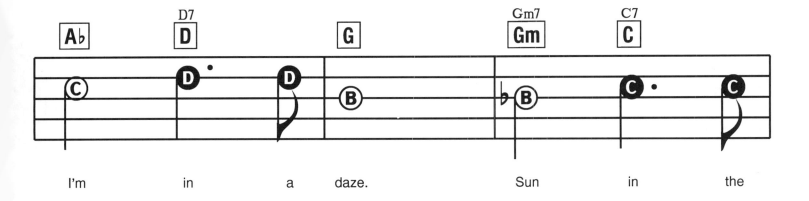

I'm in a daze. Sun in the

16

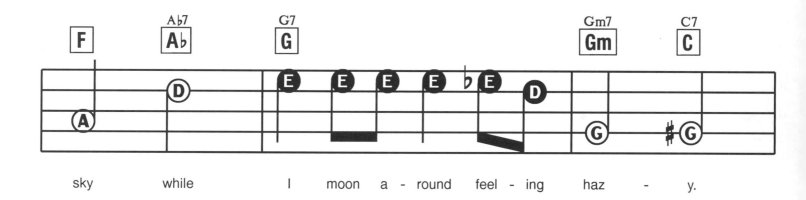

sky   while   I   moon a - round feel - ing haz -   y.

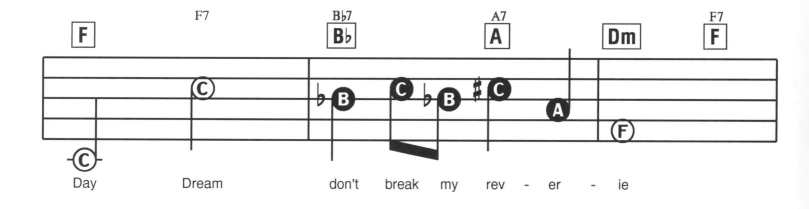

Day   Dream   don't break my rev - er - ie

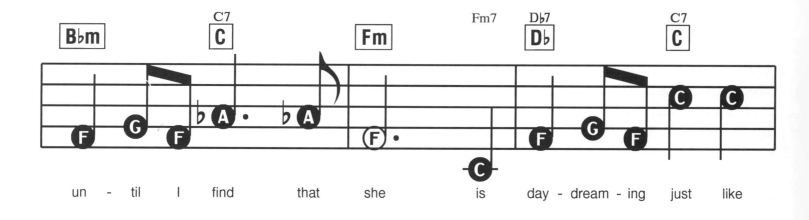

un - til I find   that she   is day - dream - ing just like

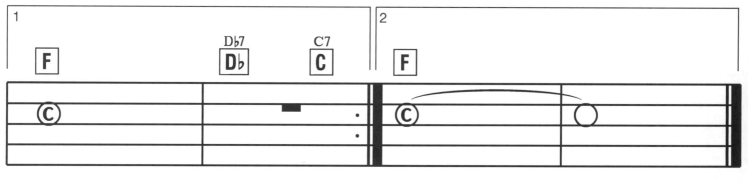

me.   me. _____

Don't Get Around Much Anymore

Registration 5
Rhythm: Fox Trot or Swing

Words and Music by Bob Russell
and Duke Ellington

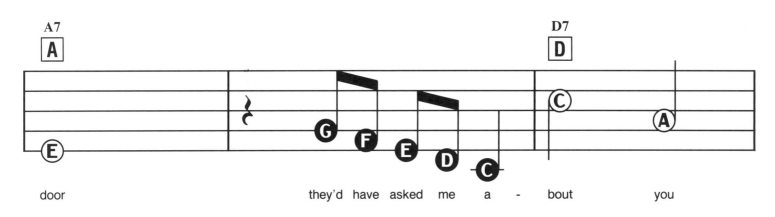

door — they'd have asked me a - bout you

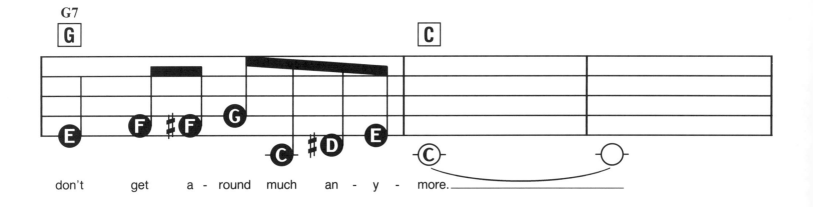

don't get a - round much an - y - more._____

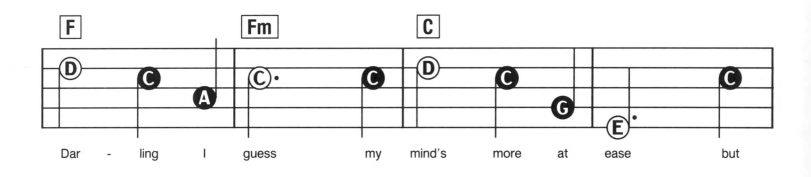

Dar - ling I guess my mind's more at ease but

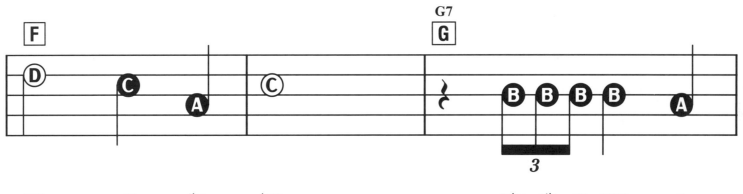

nev - er - the - less why stir up mem - o -

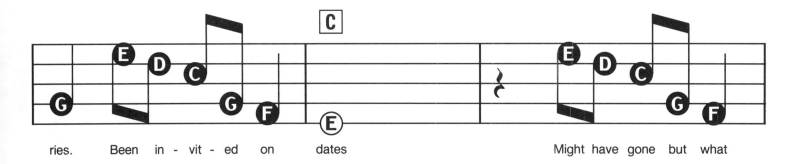

ries. Been in - vit - ed on dates Might have gone but what

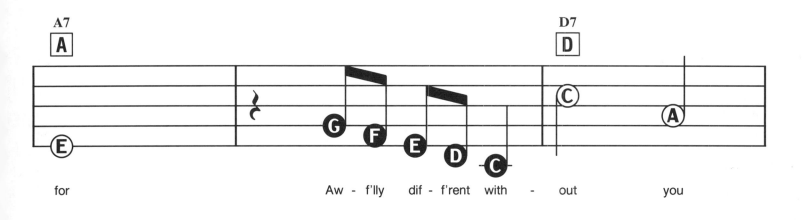

for Aw - f'lly dif - f'rent with - out you

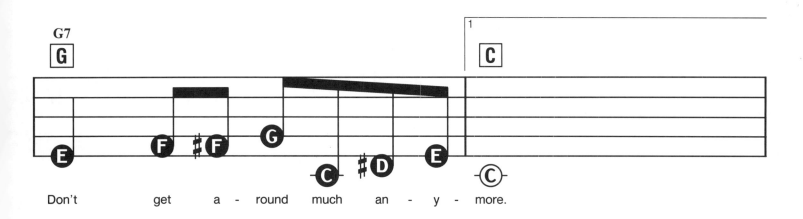

Don't get a - round much an - y - more.

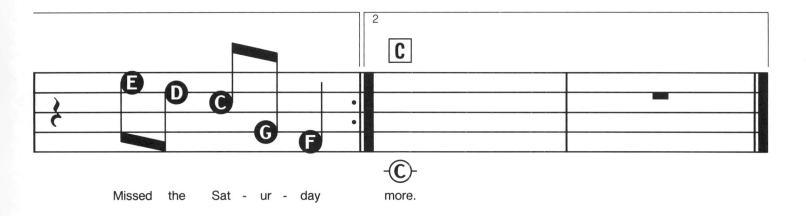

Missed the Sat - ur - day more.

Do Nothin' Till You Hear From Me

Registration 7
Rhythm: Swing

Words and Music by Bob Russell
and Duke Ellington

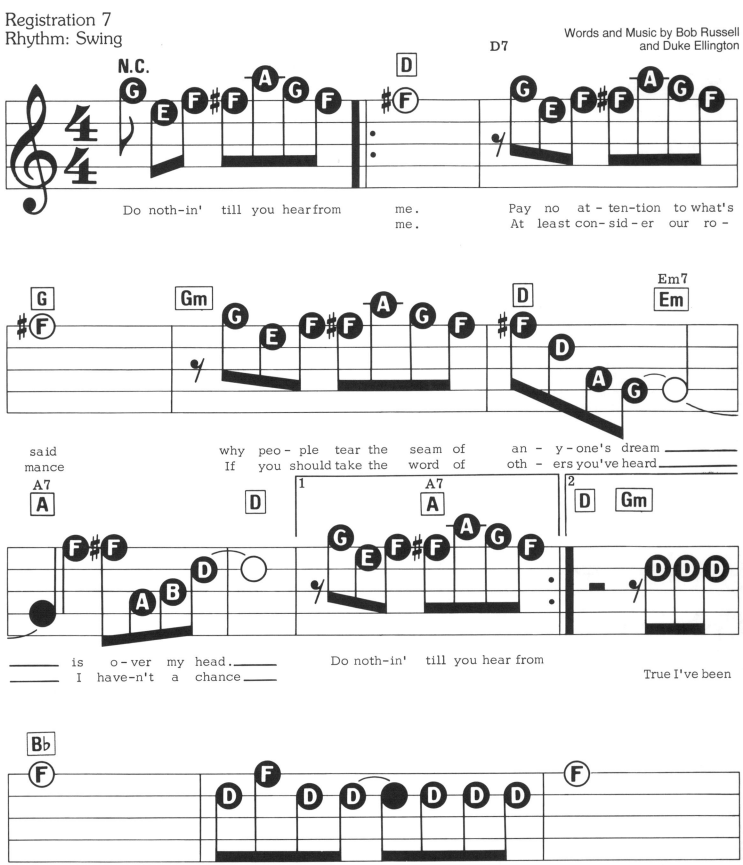

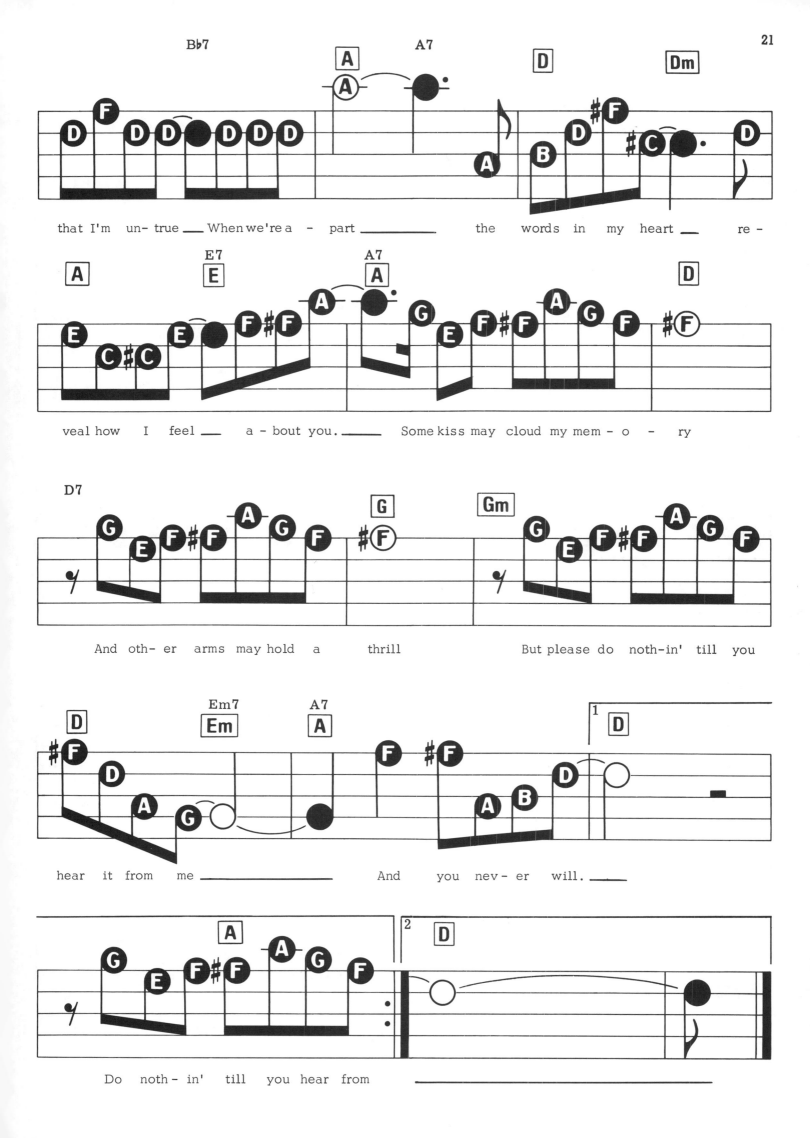

East St. Louis Toodle-Oo

Registration 7
Rhythm: March

By Duke Ellington
and Bub Miley

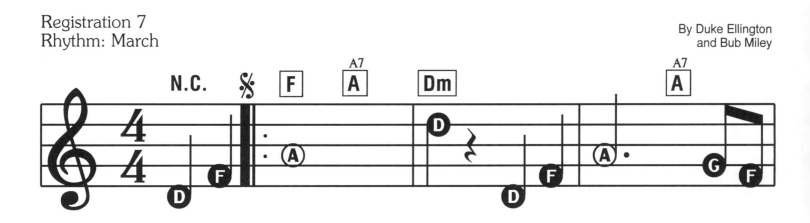

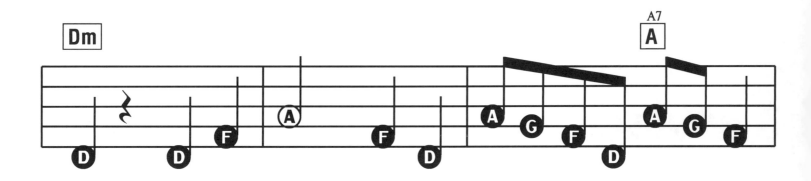

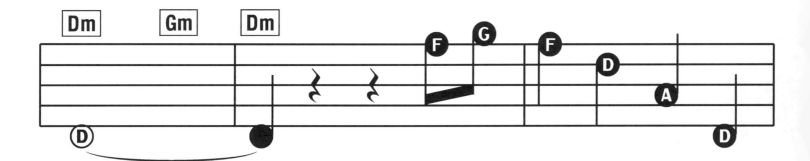

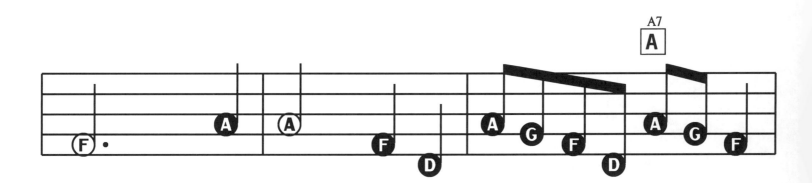

23

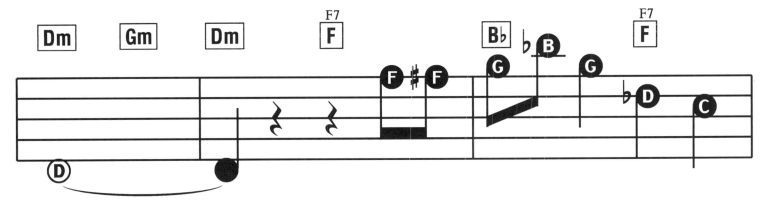

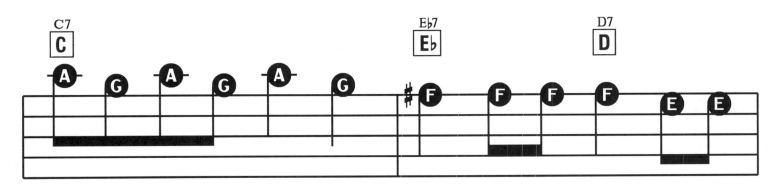

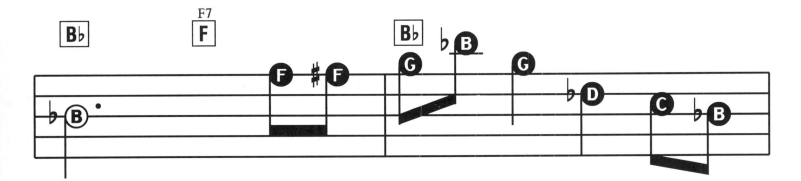

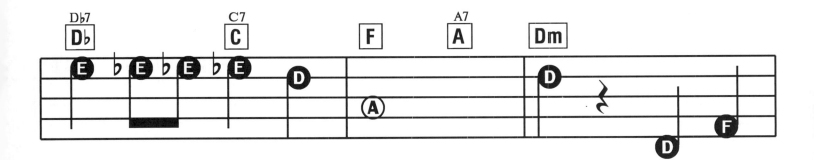

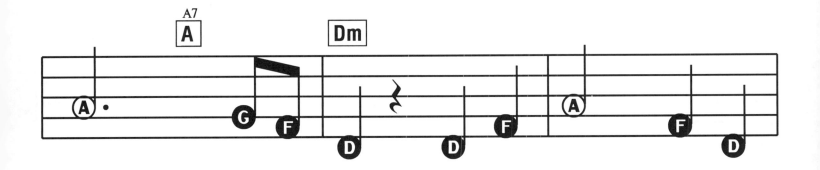

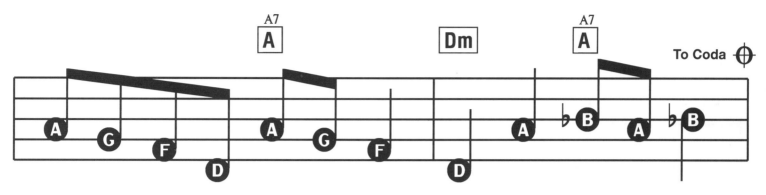

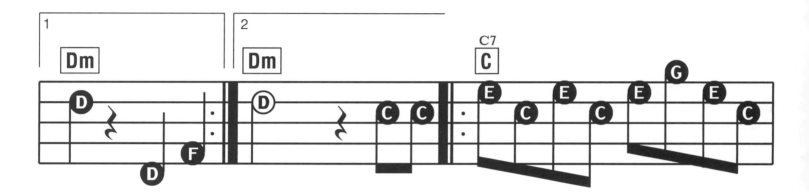

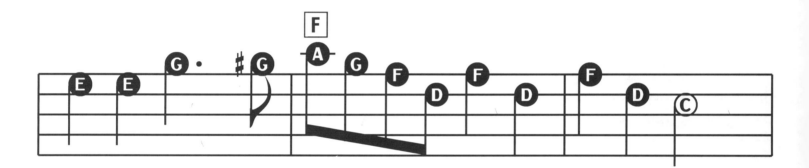

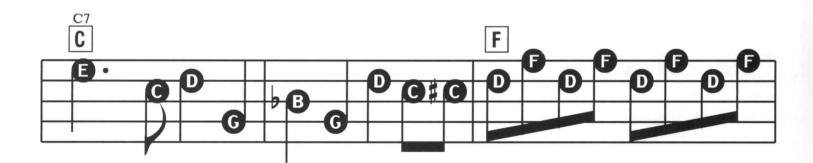

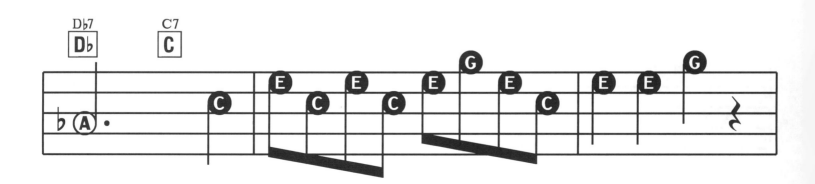

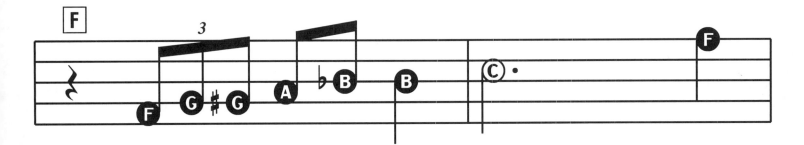

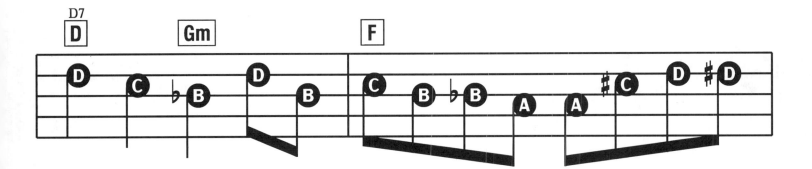

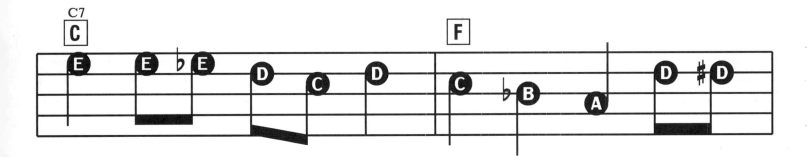

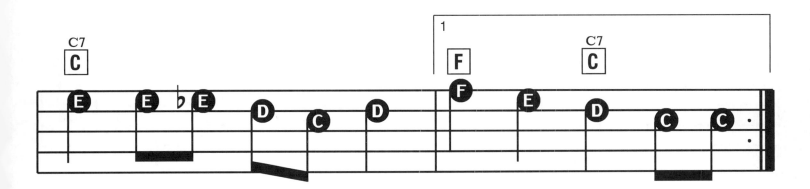

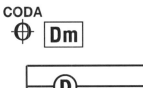

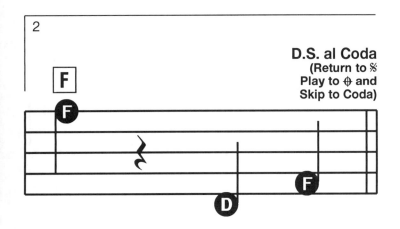

D.S. al Coda
(Return to %
Play to ⊕ and
Skip to Coda)

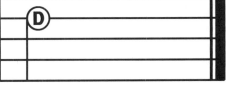

I Got It Bad And That Ain't Good

Registration 6
Rhythm: Ballad

Words by Paul Francis Webster
Music by Duke Ellington

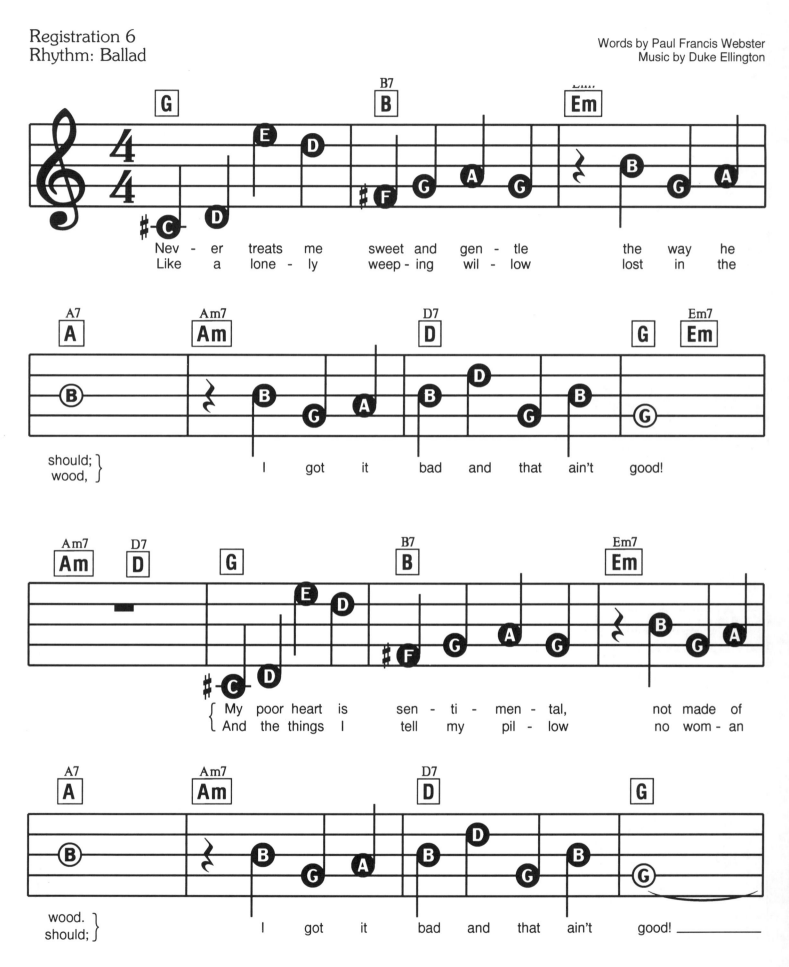

I Let A Song Go Out Of My Heart

Registration 7
Rhythm: Swing or Fox Trot

Words and Music by Duke Ellington, Henry Nemo,
John Redmond and Irving Mills

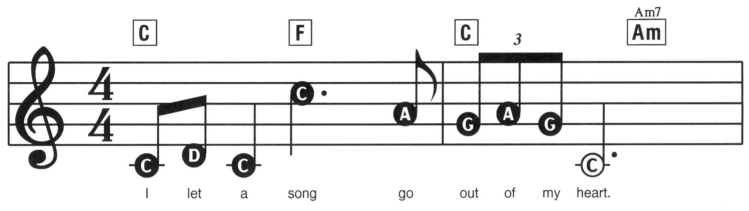

I let a song go out of my heart.

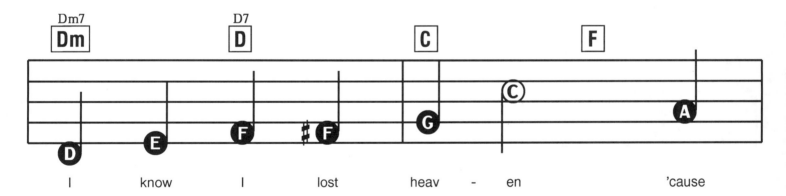

It was the sweet - est mel - o - dy.

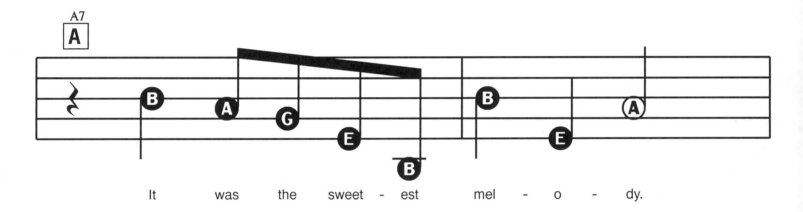

I know I lost heav - en 'cause

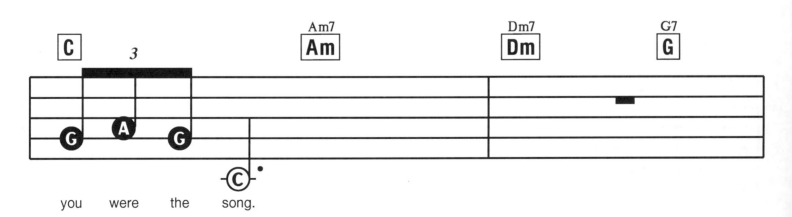

you were the song.

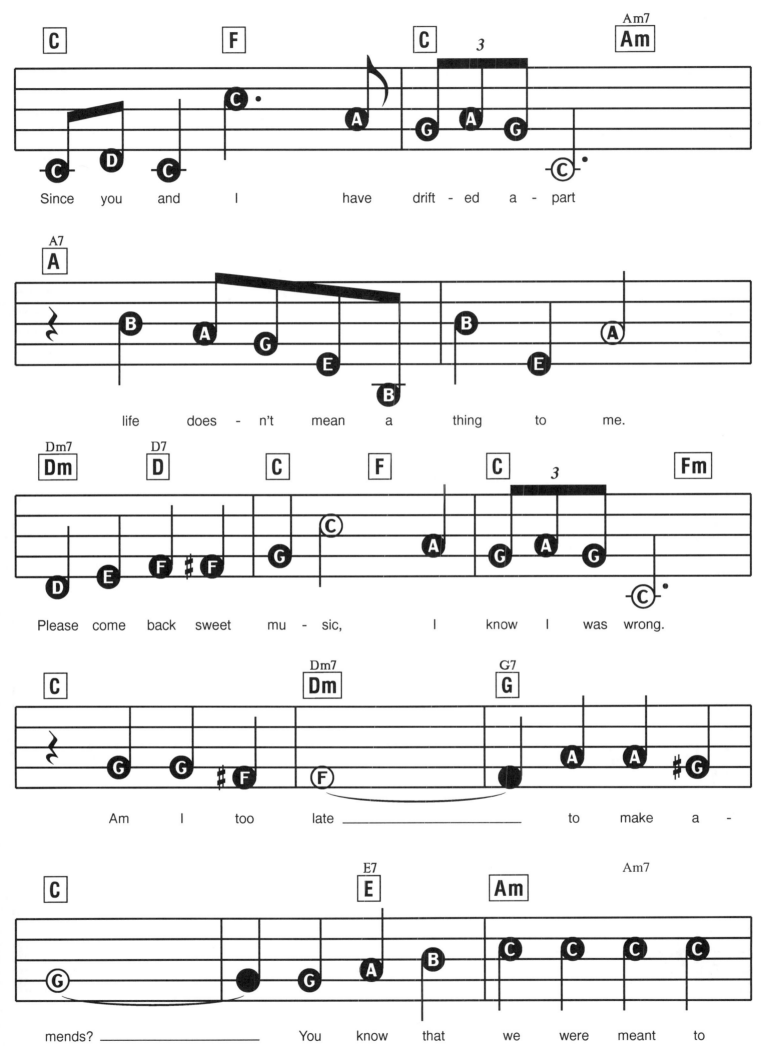

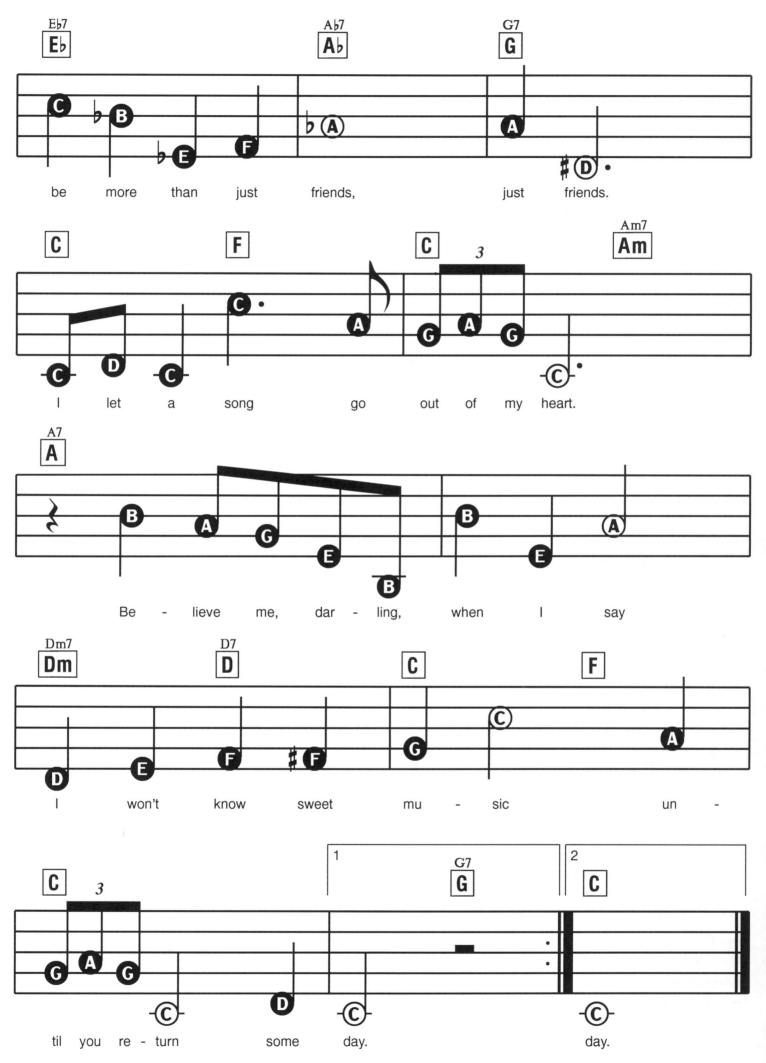

I'm Just A Lucky So And So

Registration 7
Rhythm: Swing or Fox Trot

Words by Mack David
Music by Duke Ellington

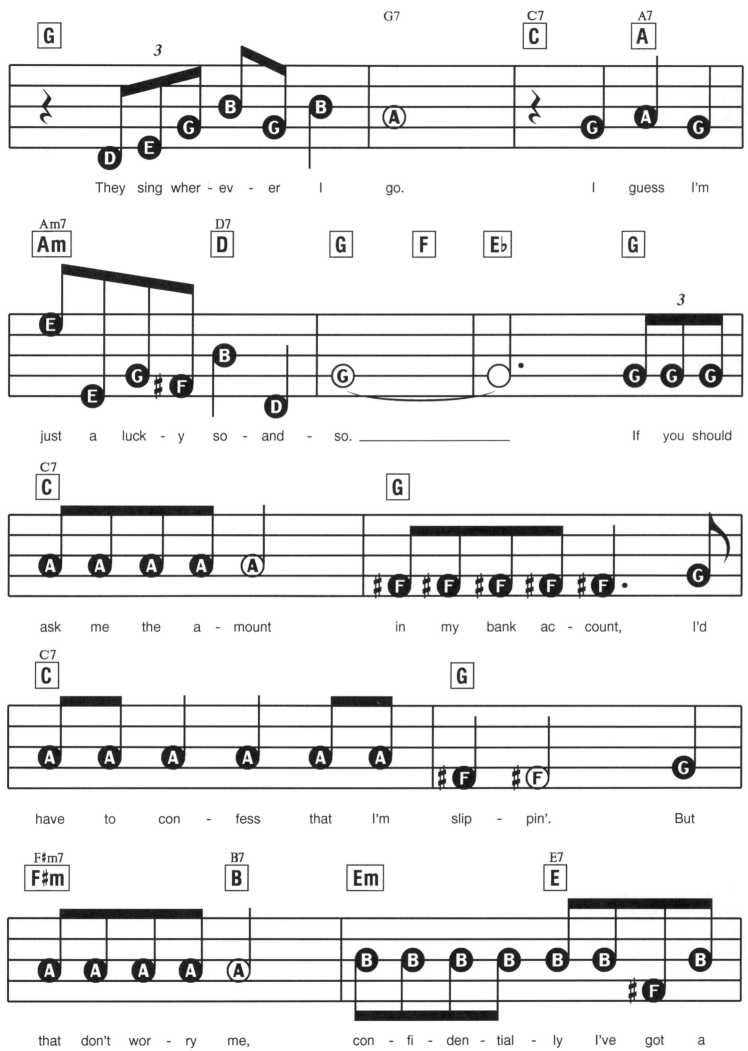

dream   that's a pip - pin'.

And when the day is through,   each night I hur - ry to

a home where love waits I   know.

I guess I'm just a luck - y so - and - so. _____

so. _____

In A Sentimental Mood

Registration 1
Rhythm: Swing

Words and Music by Duke Ellington,
Irving Mills and Manny Kurtz

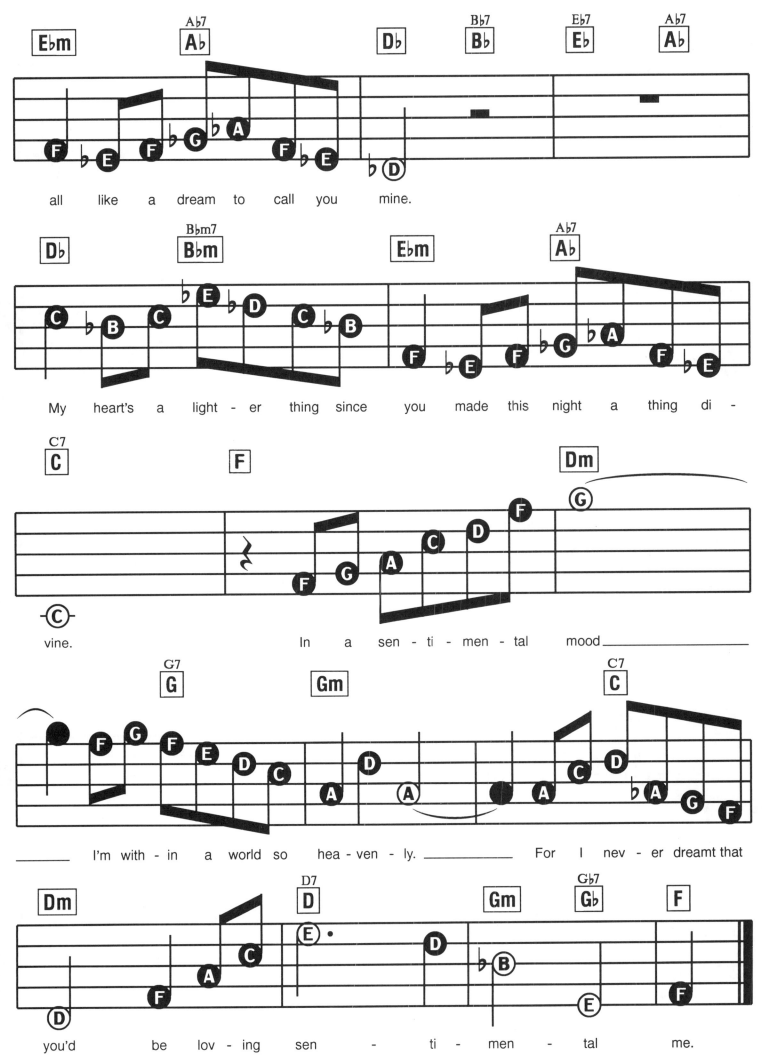

It Don't Mean A Thing
(If It Ain't Got That Swing)

Registration 7
Rhythm: Swing

Words and Music by Duke Ellington
and Irving Mills

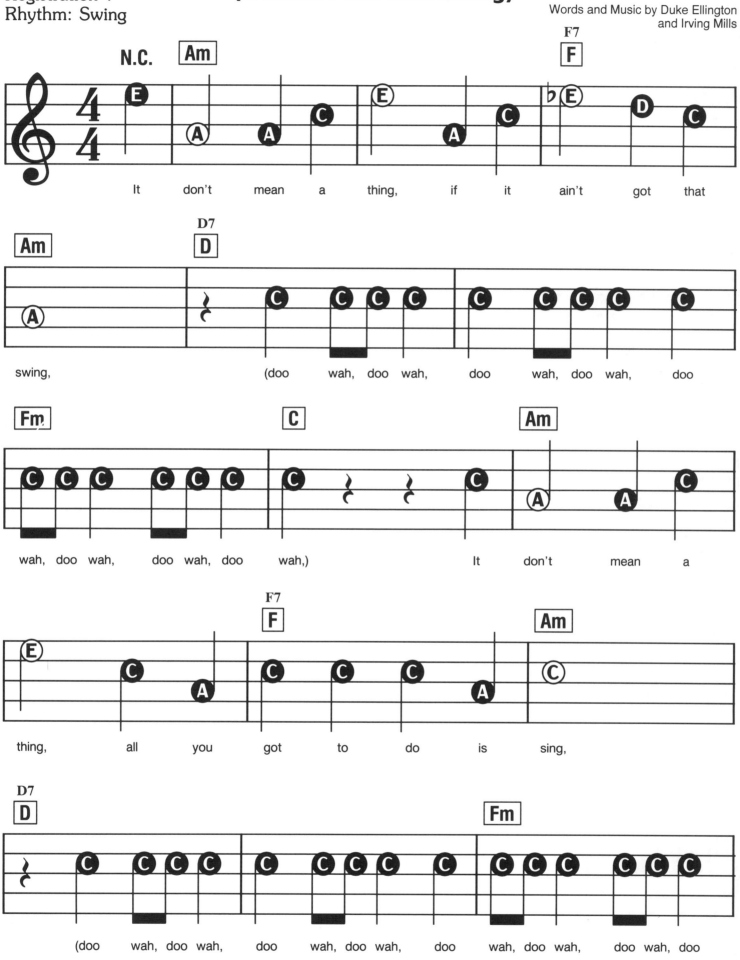

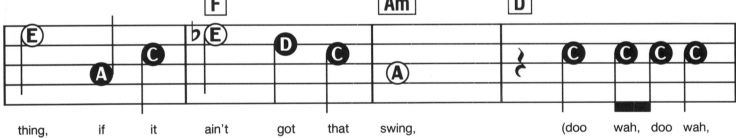

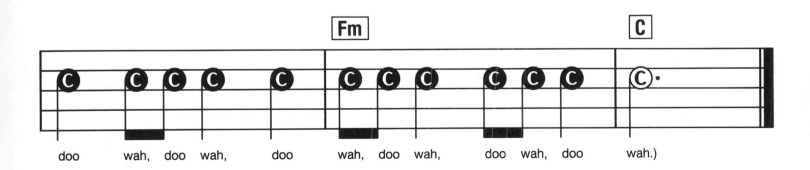

Just Squeeze Me
(But Don't Tease Me)

Registration 7
Rhythm: Swing or Fox Trot

Words by Lee Gaines
Music by Duke Ellington

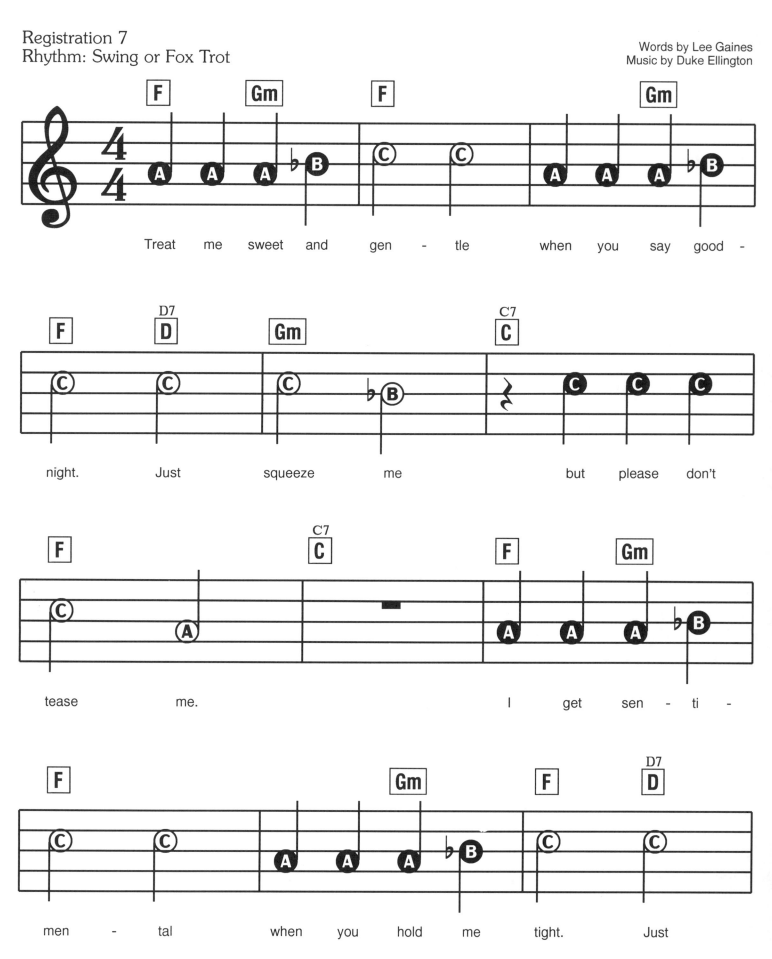

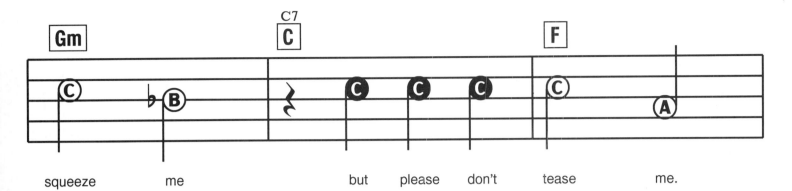

squeeze me but please don't tease me.

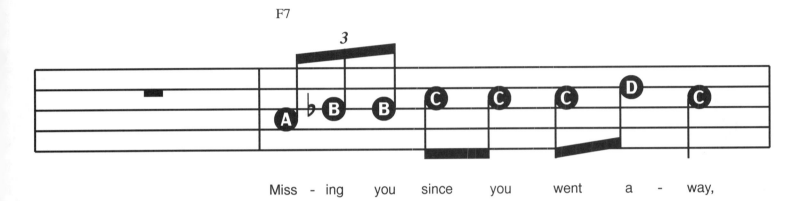

Miss - ing you since you went a - way,

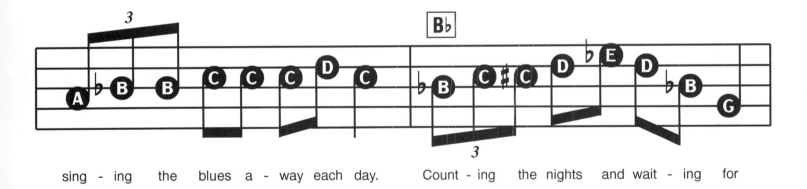

sing - ing the blues a - way each day. Count - ing the nights and wait - ing for

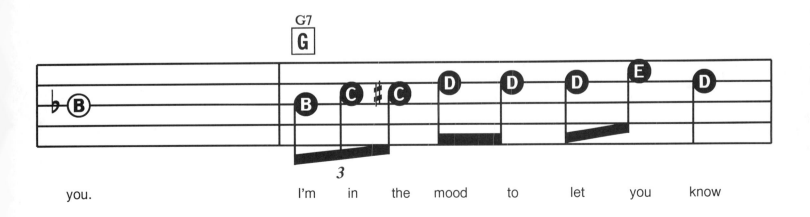

you. I'm in the mood to let you know

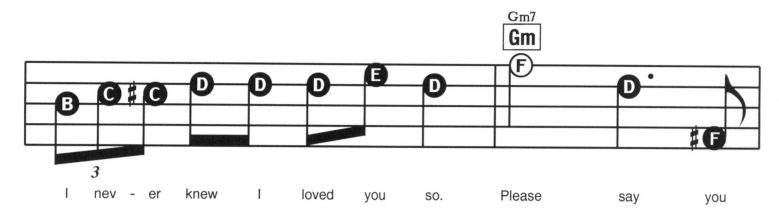

I nev - er knew I loved you so. Please say you

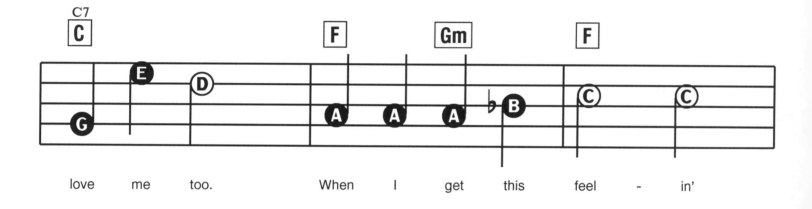

love me too. When I get this feel - in'

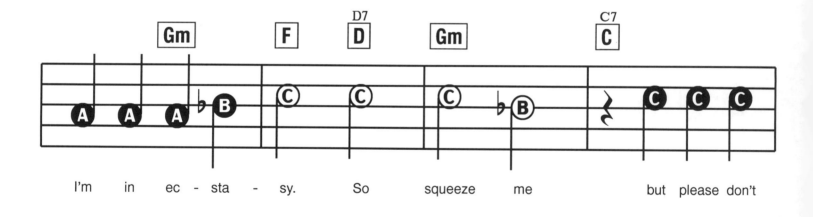

I'm in ec - sta - sy. So squeeze me but please don't

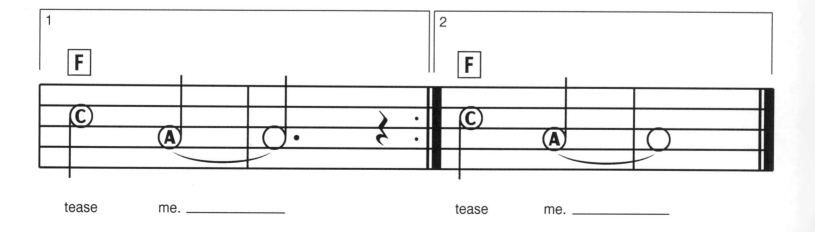

tease me. _____ tease me. _____

Love You Madly

Registration 4
Rhythm: Swing or Fox Trot

By Duke Ellington

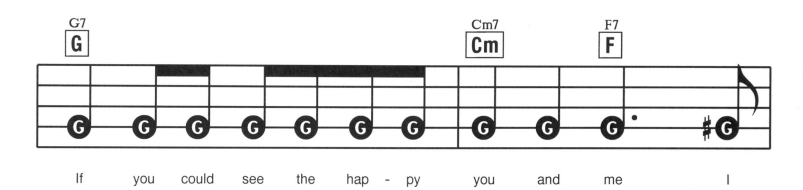

If you could see the hap - py you and me I

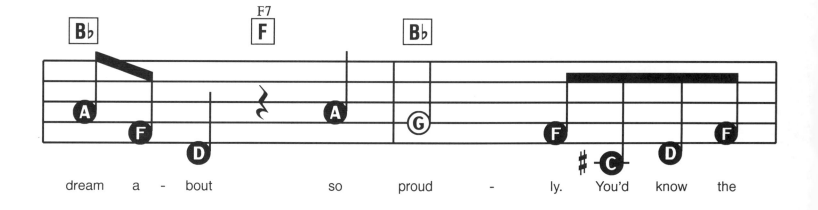

dream a - bout so proud - ly. You'd know the

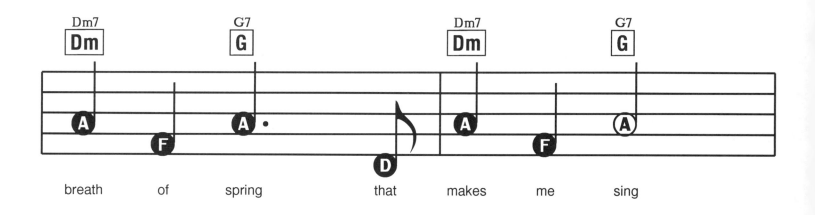

breath of spring that makes me sing

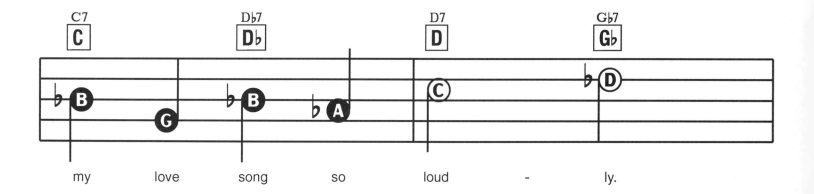

my love song so loud - ly.

43

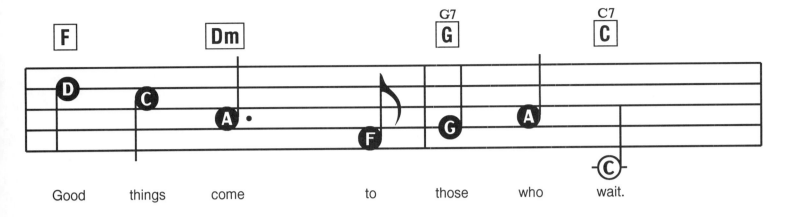

Good things come to those who wait.

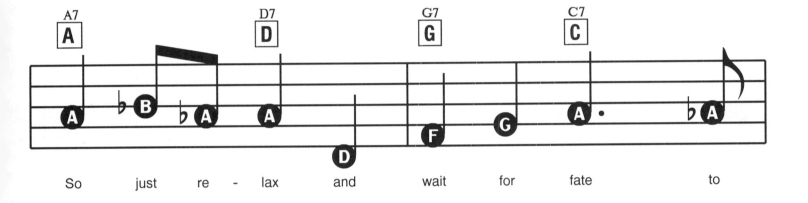

So just re - lax and wait for fate to

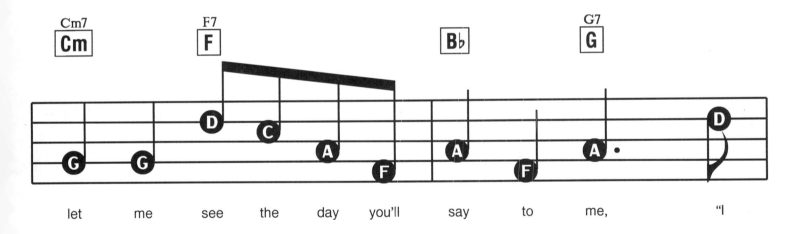

let me see the day you'll say to me, "I

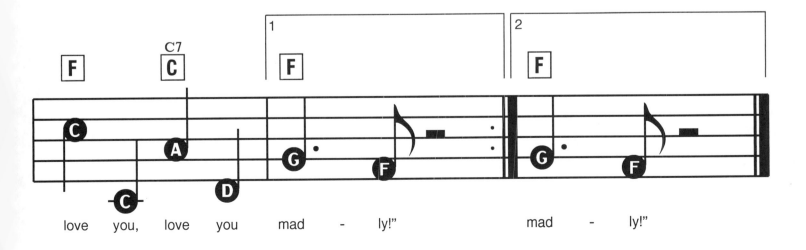

love you, love you mad - ly!" mad - ly!"

Mood Indigo

Registration 4
Rhythm: Swing or Ballad

Words and Music by Duke Ellington,
Irving Mills and Albany Bigard

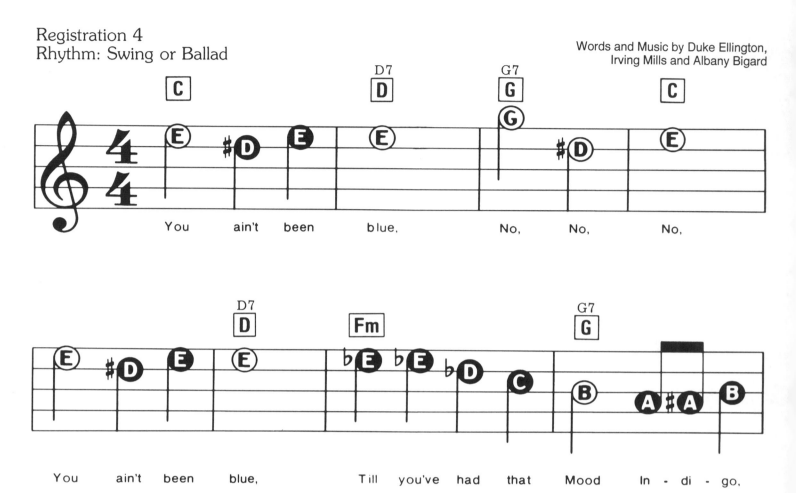

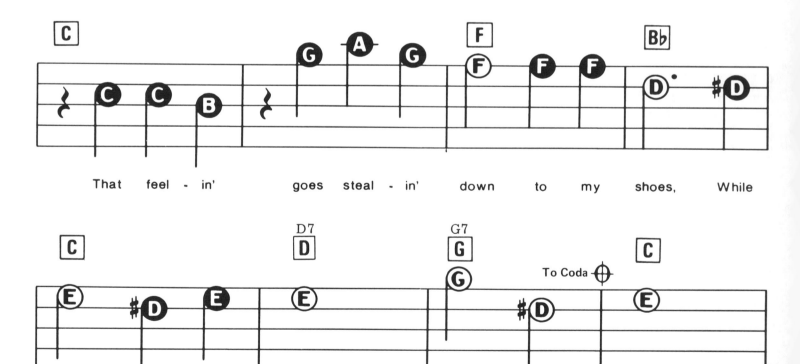

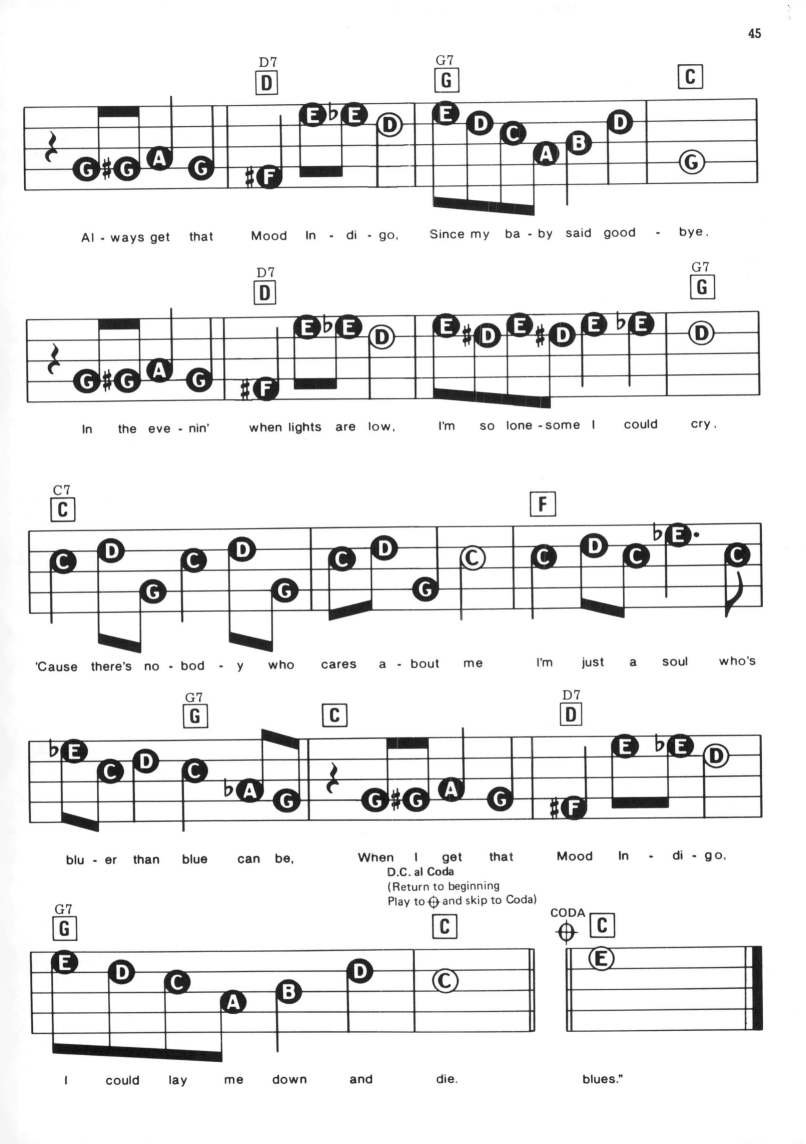

Prelude To A Kiss

Registration 7
Rhythm: Ballad

Words by Irving Gordon and Irving Mills
Music by Duke Ellington

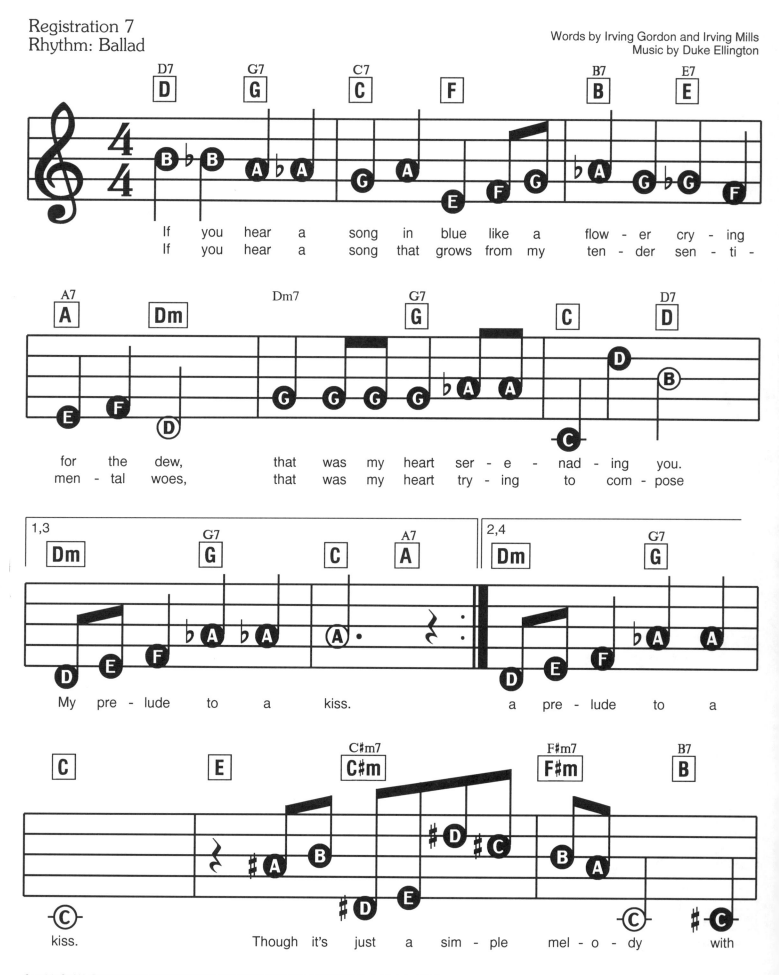

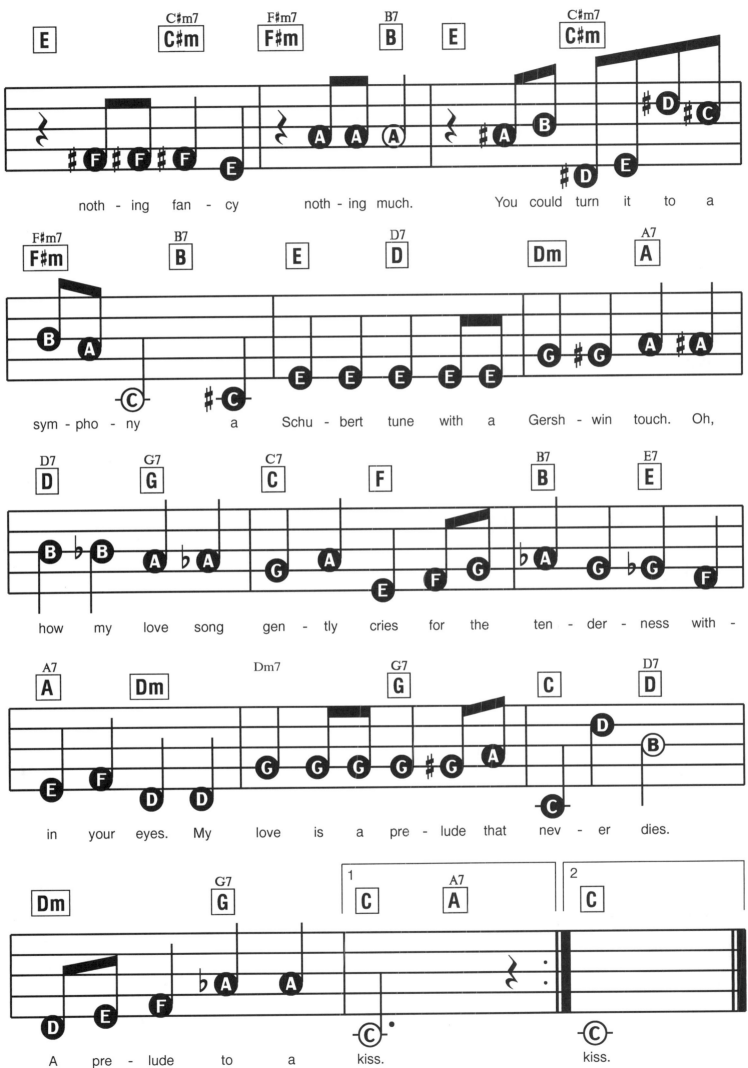

Ring Dem Bells

Registration 4
Rhythm: March

Words and Music by Duke Ellington
and Irving Mills

Solitude

Registration 7
Rhythm: Ballad

Words and Music by Duke Ellington,
Eddie De Lange and Irving Mills

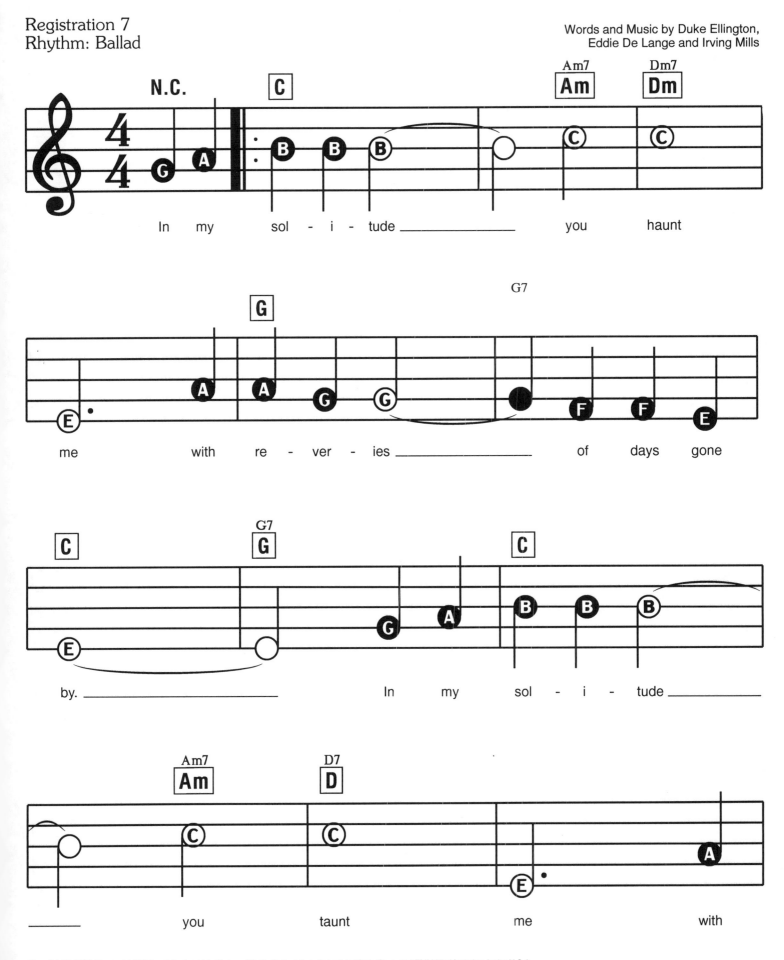

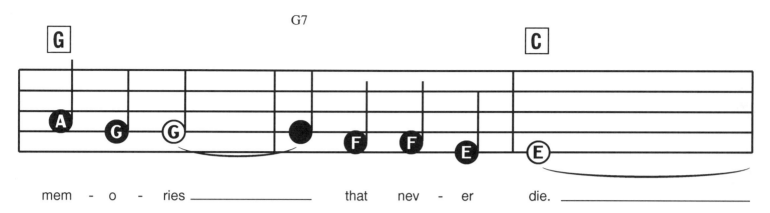

mem - o - ries _____ that nev - er die. _____

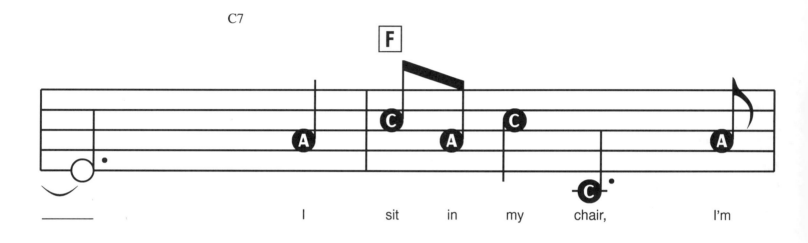

_____ I sit in my chair, I'm

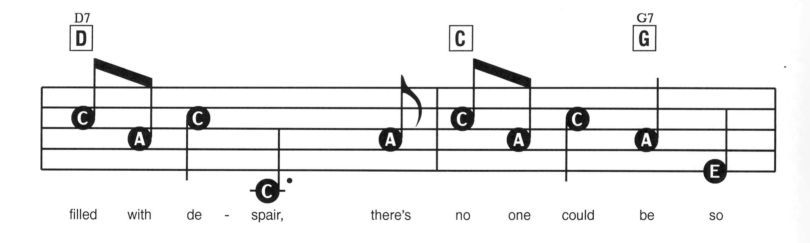

filled with de - spair, there's no one could be so

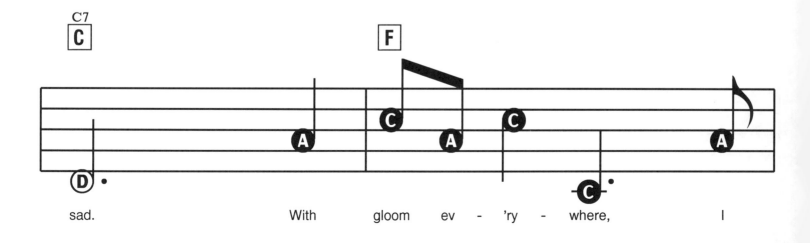

sad. With gloom ev - 'ry - where, I

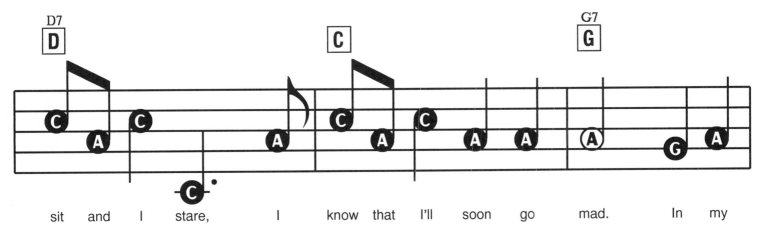

sit and I stare, I know that I'll soon go mad. In my

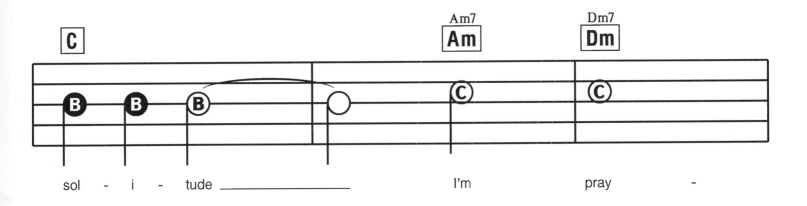

sol - i - tude _____ I'm pray -

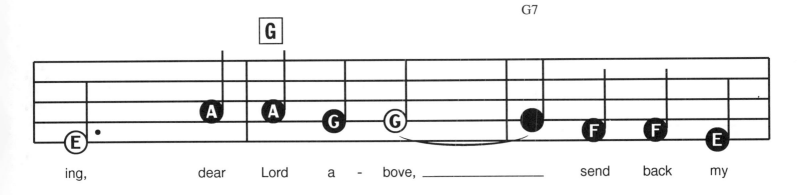

ing, dear Lord a - bove, _____ send back my

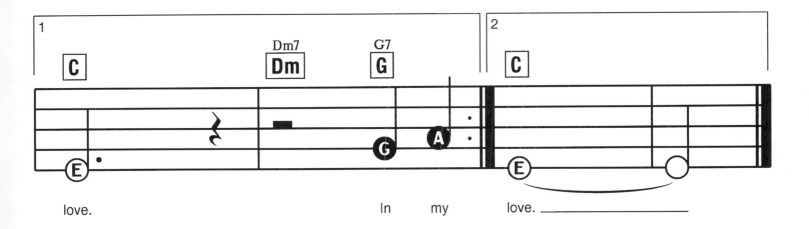

love. In my love. _____

Satin Doll

Registration 4
Rhythm: Swing or Jazz

Words by Johnny Mercer
Music by Billy Strayhorn and Duke Ellington

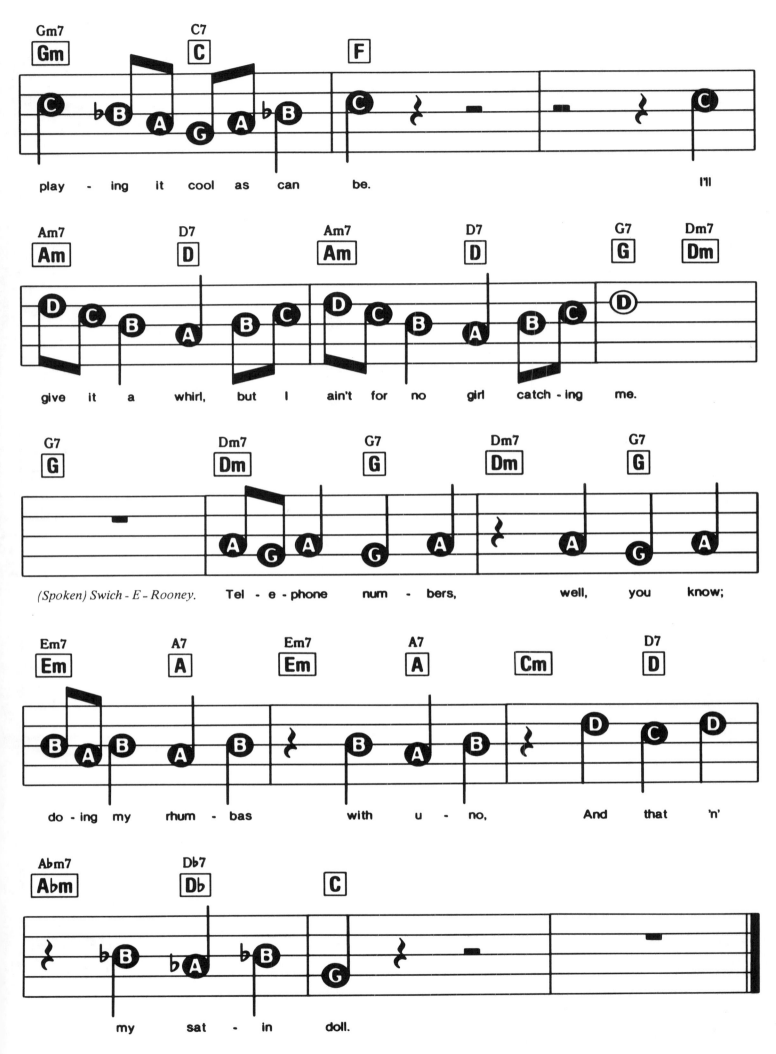

Sophisticated Lady

Registration 7
Rhythm: Fox Trot or Swing

Words and Music by Duke Ellington,
Irving Mills and Mitchell Parish

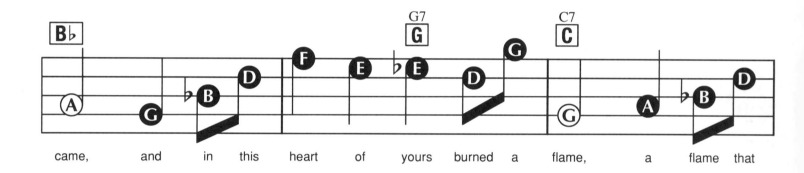

They say in - to your ear - ly life ro - mance

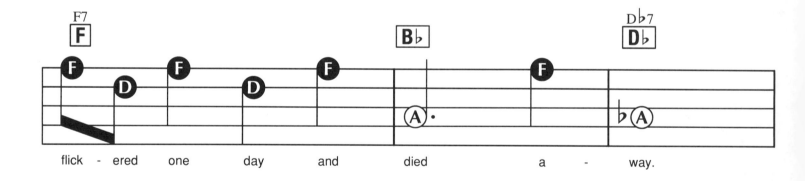

came, and in this heart of yours burned a flame, a flame that

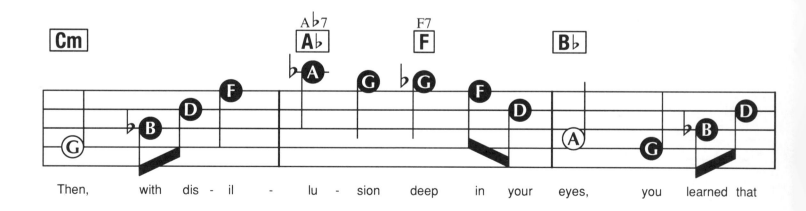

flick - ered one day and died a - way.

Then, with dis - il - lu - sion deep in your eyes, you learned that

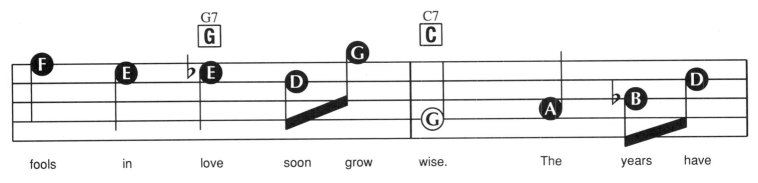

fools in love soon grow wise. The years have

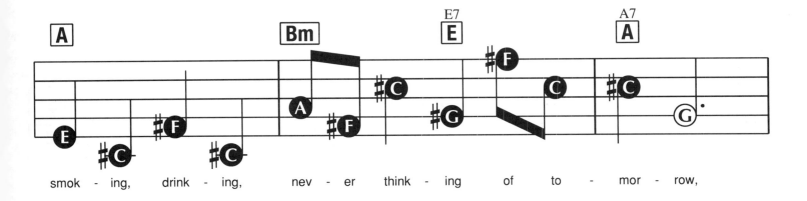

changed you, some - how; I see you now _____

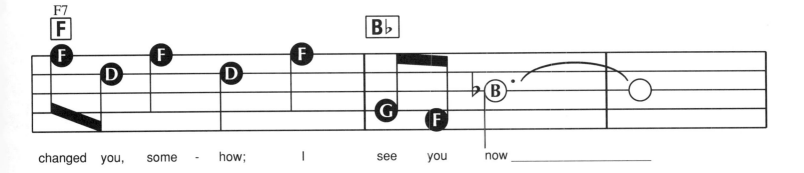

smok - ing, drink - ing, nev - er think - ing of to - mor - row,

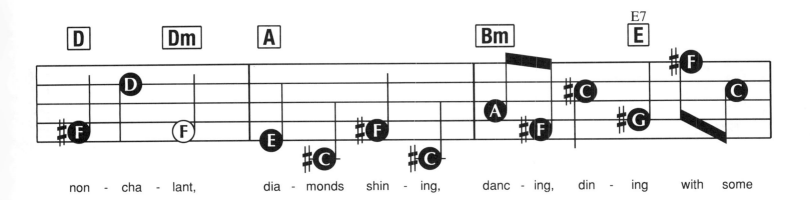

non - cha - lant, dia - monds shin - ing, danc - ing, din - ing with some

56

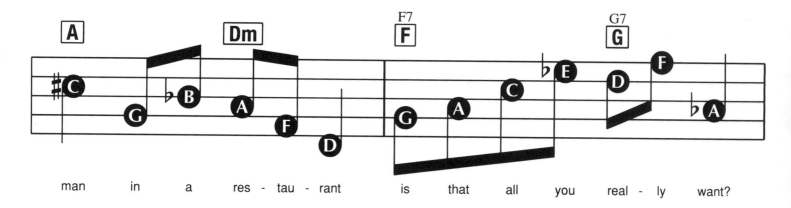

man in a res - tau - rant is that all you real - ly want?

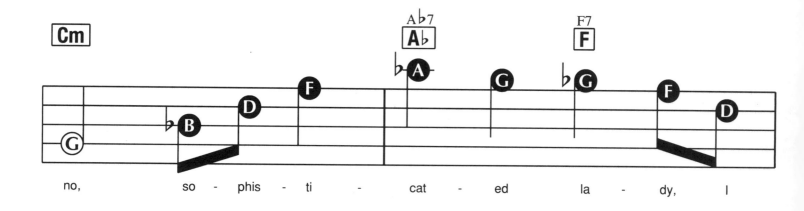

no, so - phis - ti - cat - ed la - dy, I

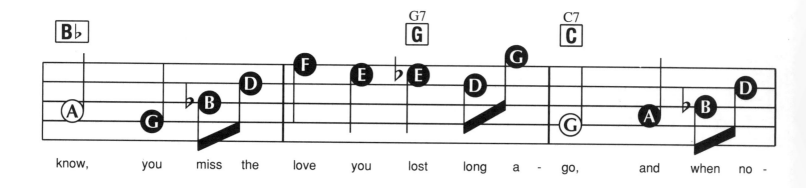

know, you miss the love you lost long a - go, and when no -

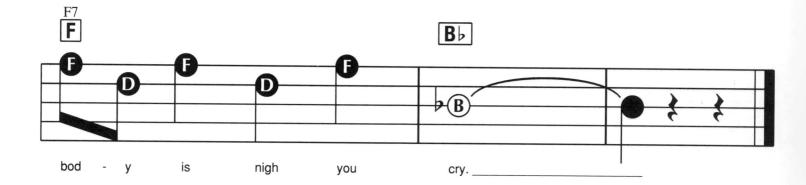

bod - y is nigh you cry. _____